Christmas in Sweden

by Cheryl L. Enderlein

Content Consultant:
Annette Lernvik-Djupström
American Swedish Institute

Hilltop Books

An Imprint of Franklin Watts
A Division of Grolier Publishing
New York   London   Hong Kong   Sydney
Danbury, Connecticut

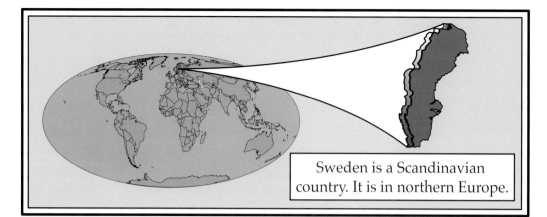

Sweden is a Scandinavian country. It is in northern Europe.

Hilltop Books
http://publishing.grolier.com
Copyright © 1998 by Capstone Press • All rights reserved
Published simultaneously in Canada• Printed in the United States of America

Library of Congress Cataloging-in-Publication Data
Enderlein, Cheryl L.
    Christmas in Sweden/by Cheryl L. Enderlein.
    p. cm.--(Christmas around the world)
    Includes bibliographical references and index.
    Summary: Describes the customs, songs, foods, and activities associated with the celebration of Christmas in Sweden.
    ISBN 1-56065-575-5
    1. Christmas--Sweden--Juvenile literature. 2. Sweden--Social life and customs--Juvenile literature. [1. Christmas--Sweden. 2. Sweden--Social life and customs.] I. Title. II. Series.
GT4987.6.E53   1998
394.2663'09485--dc21

                97-9401
                CIP
                AC

Photo credits
FPG/Ulf Sjostedt, 4
Megapix, 16; Thomas Carlgren, 14
Nordiska Museets, 20
Tiofoto/Per-Olle Stackman, 6; Lena Paterson, 8; Hans Hammarskiold, 10;
  Frank Chmura, 12; Anders Qwarnstrom, 18; Hans Andersson, 22
Unicorn Stock/Joel Dexter, cover

Table of Contents

Christmas in Sweden

Christmas is a holiday that is celebrated around the world. Celebrate means to do something enjoyable on a special occasion. People in different countries celebrate Christmas in different ways.

Sweden is a Scandinavian country. Scandinavia is an area of northern Europe. People from Sweden are called Swedes. They speak Swedish. Their Christmas greeting is God Jul (GUDT YOOL). It means Good Christmas.

Christmas Day is always celebrated on December 25. But Christmas starts early in Sweden. It begins four Sundays before Christmas. This is called Advent. Christmas lasts until Saint Knut's Day on January 13.

The weather in Sweden at Christmas is dark and snowy. There are only a few hours of sun each day. The snowy weather can last for half of the year.

Swedes celebrate special days during the Christmas season.

The First Christmas

Many Christmas celebrations are part of the Christian religion. A religion is a set of beliefs people follow. Christians are people who follow the teachings of Jesus Christ. They celebrate Christmas as Jesus' birthday.

Jesus' mother was Mary. She was married to Joseph. Mary and Joseph traveled to the city of Bethlehem. They could not find any room at the inns. An inn is like a hotel. Mary and Joseph had to stay in a stable. A stable is where animals are kept.

Jesus was born in the stable. His first bed was a manger. A manger is a food box for animals. The manger was filled with straw.

Wise men brought gifts for Jesus. They followed a bright star. The star led them to Jesus.

Many Christmas celebrations remind people of the first Christmas. Many celebrations in Sweden are Christian.

Swedes set up figures to remember the Christmas story.

Symbols of Christmas

The Star of Advent is an important Christmas symbol in Sweden. A symbol is something that stands for another thing. The Star of Advent reminds many Swedes of the star the wise men followed.

Almost every house has Stars of Advent hanging in the windows. Each star is made out of straw or thin wood. A lamp is put inside. Swedes turn the lamp on as soon as it is dark. They turn it off when they go to bed.

Advent candleholders are also important in Sweden. The holder is made of brass or wood. It holds four candles. One candle is lit on each of the four Sundays of Advent.

Many Swedes put wreaths on their doors. A wreath is a circle of branches that are twisted together. The branches are usually made out of evergreens. An evergreen is a plant that stays green all the time.

An Advent candleholder is an important symbol in Sweden.

Christmas Celebrations

Swedes celebrate Saint Lucia Day on December 13. A saint is a special person in the church. Lucia lived a long time ago. She was a Christian who served others. Almost everyone in Sweden celebrates Saint Lucia Day.

Swedish families celebrate Saint Lucia Day at home. The oldest daughter wakes up early. She puts on a long white dress and red belt. She wears a special crown of candles. She takes food to the rest of her family.

Every community also votes for a girl to play Lucia. There is a parade on Saint Lucia Day. The girl picked to be Lucia leads. She is followed by a group of girls in white dresses. She is also followed by a number of Star Boys. The Star Boys wear white shirts. They wear pointed hats with stars on them. They carry long sticks with stars on the tops.

On Saint Lucia Day, Swedish girls dress up as Lucia. Swedish boys dress up as Star Boys.

Decorations

People in Sweden decorate their houses for Christmas. Straw is one important decoration. Swedish children make ornaments out of straw. Ornaments are decorations usually hung on a Christmas tree. The ornaments might be stars, animals, or angels.

Straw reminds Swedes that Jesus was born in a stable. Some people think that straw is magical. Sometimes farmers put straw on their crops. They believe this makes the plants grow better.

At Christmas, Swedish children have a straw goat. The goat guards the Christmas tree. Swedes think the straw goat protects them from bad things.

Heart-shaped baskets are another popular kind of ornament. Swedish people fill the baskets with candy. They also put apples and Swedish flags on their trees.

A straw goat guards the family Christmas tree in Sweden.

Santa Claus

The first Santa Claus was a man named Saint Nicholas. Saint Nicholas lived a long time ago. He secretly gave gifts to children and poor people.

Today, many countries have a Christmas man like Saint Nicholas. In Sweden, the Christmas man is called Jultomten (yool-TAWM-ten).

Jultomten comes in the afternoon of Christmas Eve. Children watch for him from their windows. Jultomten has a white beard. He wears a long red coat. He carries presents for children in a big sack.

Jultomten knocks on the door of the house. He asks if there are any good children there. Jultomten is invited inside. He sits down by the Christmas tree. People offer him a drink or dessert.

Jultomten brings presents to good Swedish children.

Christmas Presents

People all over the world give gifts at Christmas. Giving gifts reminds Christians of the wise men's gifts. The wise men brought special gifts to Jesus when he was born.

Swedish people call presents julklappar (yool-KLAP-pur). They call presents julklappar because of an old tradition. A tradition is a practice continued over many years. Julklapp means to knock on the door. Long ago, people would leave a present outside someone's door. Then they would knock and run away.

Today, Jultomten hands out the julklappar. He reads the tag on each gift. The tag tells who will receive the gift. Sometimes there is a poem on the tag, too. The poem gives a hint about the present inside.

Swedish people call presents julklappar.

Holiday Foods

People in Sweden make cookies called pepparkakor (PEH-pahr-kaa-koor). Pepparkakor is a popular Christmas dessert. The cookies taste like gingerbread. They are usually shaped like hearts, stars, or goats. Sometimes people make cookie houses out of the pepparkakor.

For Christmas dinner, Swedish people have a buffet. That means all the food is set on a table. People go to the table to fill their plates. Christmas buffets have ham and pickled pigs feet. There is also dried codfish.

Swedish people also have many kinds of sweets. One of their favorite desserts is rice pudding. It is served hot with cinnamon and sugar.

Swedes make cookies called pepparkakor for Christmas dessert.

Christmas Songs

Many people in Sweden go to church on Christmas morning. The church service is very early. They sing many songs at the service.

Epiphany is celebrated on January 6. The word Epiphany means showing. Some Christians believe Jesus was shown to the wise men on this day. Long ago, Star Boys were an important part of Epiphany. They walked the streets singing songs. Star Boys are now part of Saint Lucia Day. Today, everyone in Sweden has the day off for Epiphany.

Saint Knut's Day is January 13. It is the end of the Christmas season in Sweden. Swedish people have a special song for Saint Knut's Day. People take down their Christmas trees. The children have a party. They dance around the tree in a ring dance. They sing about throwing away the tree.

Swedes dance around the tree and sing on Saint Knut's Day.

Hands On: Make a Heart-Shaped Basket

Swedish children make heart-shaped baskets to hang on their Christmas trees. They fill the baskets with candy.

What You Need

Two different colors of paper   Ruler
Pencil   Scissors

What You Do

1. Put the two pieces of paper together. That way you can cut both pieces at one time.
2. Measure your paper into strips that are three inches (eight centimeters) wide and nine inches (23 centimeters) long. Cut them out.
3. Fold the strips in half. The short ends of the strips should be together. Cut the end opposite the fold into a U shape.
4. Mark the folded edge into two parts. Each part will be one and one-half inch (four centimeters).
5. Make a cut three inches (eight centimeters) up from the mark. This will make two legs.
6. Number each leg. Use 1, 2, 3, 4.
7. Push 1 through 4. Then push 3 through 1.
8. Push 4 through 2. Then push 2 through 3. Erase the marks you can still see.
9. Fill your heart basket with candy. Put it on your tree.

Words to Know

Advent (AD-vent)—a special time to prepare for Christmas

Christian (KRISS-chuhn)—a person who follows the teachings of Jesus Christ

evergreen (EV-ur-green)—a plant that stays green all the time

inn (IN)—a place to sleep overnight like a hotel

julklappar (yool-KLAP-pur)—Swedish Christmas presents

Jultomten (yool-TAWM-ten)—Swedish Santa Claus

manger (MAYN-jur)—a food box for animals

ornament (OR-nuh-muhnt)—a decoration hung on a Christmas tree

pepparkakor (PEH-pahr-kaa-koor)—Swedish Christmas cookie like gingerbread

stable (STAY-buhl)—a building for animals like a barn

Read More

Cuyler, Margery. *The All-Around Christmas Book*. New York: Holt, Rinehart and Winston, 1982.

Fowler, Virginie. *Christmas Crafts and Customs*. Englewood Cliffs, N.J.: Prentice-Hall, 1984.

Lankford, Mary D. *Christmas Around the World*. New York: Morrow Junior Books, 1995.

Patterson, Lillie. *Christmas in Britain and Scandinavia*. Champaign, Ill.: Garrard Publishing, 1970.

Useful Addresses and Internet Sites

American Swedish Institute
2600 Park Avenue
Minneapolis, MN 55407

The Embassy of Sweden
1501 M Street NW
Washington, DC 20005

Christmas.com
http://www.christmas.com
Christmas 'round the World
http://www.auburn.edu/%7Evestmon/christmas.html
A Worldwide Christmas Calendar
http://www.algonet.se/~bernadot/christmas/info.html

Index